Executor's Checklist

Notification of Death

Who to notify after someone dies.

Executor's Checklist

©Lake Lee

Notifications Upon Death

When a family member passes, there are several entities that need to have legal notification of the death. You'll want to do it right away, not only because you don't want the task lingering over your head, but also because some government agencies are very slow in the process. It's good to get the wheels in motion – you don't want to prolong an already long and drawn out process any longer than necessary. There's also an increased risk of someone stealing the deceased's identity once the death announcement is made. So, getting started sooner rather than later is ideal.

It's generally best to make initial contact by phone. Then follow up with written verification, including any documents that they may need to confirm the death. Often, they will need copies of the death certificate - and if you're the executor, documents from probate court appointing you as executor or personal representative of the estate. Keep a record of all phone calls, with time, date, entity contacted and who you talked to, as well as a copy of everything you send with date sent.

Check this list to see which agencies, businesses or entities are appropriate for your situation. Do not consider this to be a complete list. There may be other organizations that are relevant to your particular situation.

There's a possibility that the funeral home may have done some of the notifications, so check with them.

GOVERNMENT AGENCIES:

- <u>State Dept of Motor Vehicles</u> (drivers license or state ID)
- _____
- _____
- _____
- _____

- <u>Veteran's Administration</u> (military or former military)
- _____
- _____
- _____
- _____

- <u>Social Security Administration</u> 800-772-1213
- _____
- _____
- _____
- _____

Notifications Upon Death

- <u>Defense Finance and Accounting Service</u> (if deceased is retired military receiving benefits).

  - _____
  - _____
  - _____
  - _____

- <u>Office of Personnel Management</u> (if deceased worked as federal civil service employee)

  - _____
  - _____
  - _____
  - _____

- <u>U.S. Citizenship and Immigration Service</u> (if deceased was not U.S. Citizen)

  - _____
  - _____
  - _____
  - _____

o <u>State/County Board of Elections</u> (if deceased was registered voter)

o _____

o _____

o _____

o _____

o <u>Other</u>

_____

_____

_____

_____

_____

_____

o <u>Other</u>

_____

_____

_____

_____

_____

_____

_____

o <u>Other</u>

_____

_____

_____

_____

_____

_____

BANKS, CREDIT CARD AND FINANCIAL INSTITUTIONS:

○ <u>Credit Card and Merchant Card Companies</u>

○ _____

○ _____

○ _____

○ <u>Banks, Savings and Loans, Credit Unions</u>

○ _____

○ _____

○ _____

○ <u>Mortgage Companies, Lenders</u>

○ _____

○ _____

○ _____

○ <u>Financial Planners/Stock Brokers</u>

○ _____

○ _____

○ _____

Notifications Upon Death

○ <u>Pension Providers</u>

○ _____

○ _____

○ _____

○ <u>Don't forget any online banks, investment and trading accounts, etc.</u>

○ _____

○ _____

○ _____

○ <u>Other</u>

_____

_____

_____

_____

○ <u>Other</u>

_____

_____

_____

_____

Notifications Upon Death

○ <u>Other</u>

_____

_____

_____

_____

○ <u>Other</u>

_____

_____

_____

_____

Worksheets - sheets that work!

INSURANCE AND ANNUITY COMPANIES:

○ <u>Life Insurance Companies</u>

○ _____

○ _____

○ _____

○ _____

○ <u>Annuity Companies</u>

○ _____

○ _____

○ _____

○ _____

○ <u>Automobile Insurance Companies</u>

○ _____

○ _____

○ _____

○ _____

Notifications Upon Death

○ <u>Health/Medical Insurance Companies</u>

  ○ _____

  ○ _____

  ○ _____

  ○ _____

○ <u>Vision/Dental Insurance Companies</u>

  ○ _____

  ○ _____

  ○ _____

  ○ _____

○ <u>Property Insurance Companies</u>

  ○ _____

  ○ _____

  ○ _____

  ○ _____

○ <u>Disability Insurance</u>

○ _____

○ _____

○ _____

○ _____

○ <u>Mutual Benefit Companies</u>

○ _____

○ _____

○ _____

○ _____

○ <u>Other</u>

○ _____

○ _____

○ _____

○ _____

○ <u>Other</u>

○ _____

○ _____

○ _____

○ _____

○ <u>Other</u>

○ _____

○ _____

○ _____

○ _____

CREDIT REPORTING BUREAUS:

Since each of the credit reporting agencies may have information from different creditors, be sure to request a credit report from each to ensure that you have a record of all possible accounts that need to be notified. Inform the three national credit reporting agencies of the death and request that they mark all accounts as "Account Holder Deceased. Account is Closed."

○ <u>Equifax Credit Reporting</u>

○ _____

○ _____

○ _____

○ <u>Experian Credit Reporting</u>

○ _____

○ _____

○ _____

○ <u>TransUnion</u>

○ _____

○ _____

○ _____

Notifications Upon Death

○ <u>Other</u>

_____

_____

○ <u>Other</u>

_____

_____

ONLINE SOCIAL MEDIA ACCOUNTS:

Visit each of the social media sites to follow their specific instructions on how to close accounts.

- ○ Facebook – Facebook.com/help
- ○ _____

- ○ Twitter – support.Twitter.com/
- ○ _____

- ○ LinkedIn – linkedin.com/help
- ○ _____

- ○ Instagram – help.Instagram.com
- ○ _____

- ○ Google/YouTube - support.google.com/accounts
- ○ _____

Notifications Upon Death

○ <u>Other</u>

_____

_____

○ <u>Other</u>

_____

_____

○ <u>Other</u>

_____

_____

○ <u>Other</u>

_____

_____

○ <u>Other</u>

_____

_____

○ <u>Other</u>

_____

_____

○ <u>Other</u>

_____

_____

○ <u>Other</u>

_____

_____

CLUBS AND MEMBERSHIPS:

○ Professional Associations and Unions

    ○ _____

    ○ _____

    ○ _____

    ○ _____

    ○ _____

○ Health, Sports, Fitness and Athletic Clubs

    ○ _____

    ○ _____

    ○ _____

    ○ _____

    ○ _____

○ Public Library

    ○ _____

    ○ _____

    ○ _____

○ <u>Civic Service Organizations:</u> Rotary, Kiwanis, Lions, Elks, Veterans, etc.

    ○ _____

    ○ _____

    ○ _____

    ○ _____

    ○ _____

○ <u>School and Alumni Organizations</u>

    ○ _____

    ○ _____

    ○ _____

    ○ _____

    ○ _____

○ <u>Automobile or RV Clubs</u>

    ○ _____

    ○ _____

    ○ _____

    ○ _____

    ○ _____

- <u>Sports or Recreational Clubs</u> (Folf, Shooting, Basketball, Gym)

  - ○ _____

  - ○ _____

  - ○ _____

  - ○ _____

  - ○ _____

- <u>Other</u>

  _____

  _____

- <u>Other</u>

  _____

  _____

DO NOT CALL/CONTACT LISTS:

Direct Marketing Association – www.ims-dm.com/cgi/ddnc

○ _____

○ _____

For a small fee, you can list the deceased's name on a Deceased List. Members of the Direct Marketing Association will delete the name from their mailing lists.

Disclaimer:

(1) Introduction

This disclaimer governs the use of this report. [By using this report, you accept this disclaimer in full.]

(2) Credit

This disclaimer was created using a seq legal template.

(3) No advice

The report contains information about what to do when you are responsible for notification upon the death of someone. Do not consider this information to be complete and exhaustive. It is not. Every person's circumstances are different, and it is impossible to include everything that should be considered. This is merely a starting point for you to consider.

The information is not advice and should not be treated as such. You must not rely on the information in the report as an alternative to legal / medical / financial / taxation / accounting advice from an appropriately qualified professional. If you have any specific questions about any legal / medical / financial / taxation / accounting matter you should consult an appropriately qualified professional. You should never delay seeking legal advice, disregard legal advice, or commence or discontinue any legal action because of information in this report.

(4) No representations or warranties

To the maximum extent permitted by applicable law and subject to section 6 below, we exclude all representations, warranties, undertakings and guarantees relating to the report. Without prejudice to the generality of the foregoing paragraph, we do not represent, warrant, undertake or guarantee:
A) That the information in the report is correct, accurate, complete or non-misleading;
B) That the use of guidance in the report will lead to any particular outcome or result; or
 C) In particular, that by using the guidance in the report you will have all of the information you need to complete your task of death notification.

(5) Limitations and exclusions of liability

The limitations and exclusions of liability set out in this section and elsewhere in this disclaimer are subject to section 6 below, and govern all liabilities arising under the disclaimer or in relation to the report, including liabilities arising in contract, in tort (including negligence) and for breach of statutory duty.

We will not be liable to you with respect to or regarding any losses arising out of any event or events beyond our reasonable control. We will not be liable to you with respect to or regarding any business losses, including without limitation, loss of or damage to profits, income, revenue, use, production, anticipated savings, business, contracts, commercial opportunities or goodwill. We will not be liable to you with respect to or regarding any loss or corruption of any data, database or software. We will not be liable to you with respect to or regarding any special, indirect or consequential loss or damage.

(6) Exceptions

Nothing in this disclaimer shall: limit or exclude our liability for death or personal injury resulting from negligence; limit or exclude our liability for fraud or fraudulent misrepresentation; limit any of our liabilities in any way that is not permitted under applicable law; or exclude any of our liabilities that may not be excluded under applicable law.

(7) Severability

If a section of this disclaimer is determined by any court or other competent authority to be unlawful and/or unenforceable, the other sections of this disclaimer continue in effect. If any unlawful and/or unenforceable section would be lawful or enforceable if part of it were deleted, that part will be deemed to be deleted, and the rest of the section will continue in effect.

(8) Law and jurisdiction

This disclaimer will be governed by and construed in accordance with United States law, and any disputes relating to this disclaimer will be subject to the exclusive jurisdiction of the courts of the state of Montana, USA.